discovermore
Your Government

T0026775

Paying Taxes

Ezra E. Knopp

Britannica
Educational Publishing

IN ASSOCIATION WITH

R THE ROSEN
PUBLISHING
GROUP

Published in 2024 by Britannica Educational Publishing (a trademark of Encyclopædia Britannica, Inc.) in association with The Rosen Publishing Group, Inc.
2544 Clinton Street, Buffalo, NY 14224

Distributed exclusively by Rosen Publishing.
To see additional Britannica Educational Publishing titles, go to rosenpublishing.com.

Editor: Caitie McAneney
Book Design: Rachel Rising

Photo Credits: Cover; (series back ground) Dai Yim/Shutterstock.com; Cover, IhorL/Shutterstock.com; p. 4 BearFotos/Shutterstock.com; p. 5 Sergey Mironov/Shutterstock.com; p. 6 Mountains Hunter/Shutterstock.com; p. 7 https://commons.wikimedia.org/wiki/File:Reeve_and_Serfs.jpg; p. 9 kavram/Shutterstock.com; p. 9 Ilia Baksheev/Shutterstock.com; p. 10 https://commons.wikimedia.org/wiki/File:A_map_of_the_British_Empire_in_North_America._LOC_74694152.jpg; p. 11 https://commons.wikimedia.org/wiki/File:The_Mayflower_at_sea_(90230).jpg; p. 12 https://commons.wikimedia.org/wiki/File:Pennsylvania_Journal,_Stamp_Act_announcement.jpg; p. 13 https://commons.wikimedia.org/wiki/File:P45_THE_STAMP_ACT_RIOTS_AT_BOSTON,_IN_AMERICA.jpg; p. 14 https://commons.wikimedia.org/wiki/File:Crispus_Attucks.jpg; p. 15 Everett Collection/Shutterstock.com; p. 16 Morphart Creation/Shutterstock.com; p. 17 Mike Flippet/Shutterstock.com; p. 18 ABCDstock/Shutterstock.com; p. 19 fongbeerredhot/Shutterstock.com; p. 20 Leonid Sorokin/Shutterstock.com; pp. 21, 24 Andrey_Popov/Shutterstock.com; p. 22 Inside Creative House/Shutterstock.com; p. 23 PopTika/Shutterstock.com; p. 25 Paul Brady Photography/Shutterstock.com; p. 26 Ringo Chiu/Shutterstock.com; p. 27 goodluz/Shutterstock.com; p. 29 alisafarov/Shutterstock.com; p. 29 Monkey Business Images/Shutterstock.com.

Cataloguing-in-Publication Data

Names: Knopp, Ezra E.
Title: Paying taxes / Ezra E. Knopp.
Description: New York : Britannica Educational Publishing, in Association with Rosen Educational Services. 2024. | Series: Discover more: your government | Includes glossary and index.
Identifiers: ISBN 9781642829082 (library bound) | ISBN 9781642829075 (pbk) | ISBN 9781642829099 (ebook)
Subjects: LCSH: Taxation--United States--Juvenile literature. | Taxation--Juvenile literature.
Classification: LCC HJ2381.K66 2024 | DDC 336.200973–dc23

Find us on

Contents

Tax Time!. 4

The First Taxes. 6

When in (Ancient) Rome. 8

The Fight for Representation 10

Stamp Act Protests 12

The Unpopular Townshend Acts 14

Intolerable Acts. .16

Taxes Are Important. 18

Taxes for Work 20

Taxes for Your Community 22

Taxes When You Shop 24

Understanding Tariffs 26

Other Ways to Raise Money 28

Glossary 30

For More Information 31

Index 32

Tax Time!

    Imagine you're spending the day walking around your community. You play in the park. You wave to a police officer keeping your neighborhood safe. You see town workers cutting down old trees and taking away trash. All of these things cost money. How does your government pay for it?

    Local governments pay for their public spaces and services with taxes. State and federal governments also use taxes to pay for things. Taxes are certain amounts of money paid by citizens.

You might notice things cost more than their price tag suggests. That's because of sales tax.

Taxes pay for important services, such as law enforcement and fire safety.

Governments get taxes in different ways. City governments ask people to pay to own a pet, get married, or park their car in certain places. State governments charge fees for driver's **licenses**. Federal governments take a part of what people earn at work. Learning about taxes will help you better understand your government and money.

WORD WISE

A license is a document, plate, or tag showing that you have permission to own or do something.

The First Taxes

Taxes aren't new. In fact, they've been around since ancient times. Back then, people sometimes gave goods or services to support their governments. One of the oldest types of taxes was for land and crops. It was called a tithe. A tithe was one-tenth of a farmer's crops or the animals he raised.

Many ancient Egyptians had to do forced work as a kind of taxation.

The word *corvée* is a French word from the 14th century, though the idea goes back much farther than that.

Another ancient tax was called the corvée (pronounced "kor-VAY"). The corvée was a type of unpaid work that poor people could do for a short time if they couldn't afford to give their government crops or money. Some people might have had to help build a road or a bridge. Some citizens might have been sent to fight in a battle. Their debt, or what they owed, was considered paid once their work was done.

In ancient times, there was a wide gap between people who owned very little land and could grow few crops and those who owned a lot of land and could grow more. How is the tithe system fair in this case?

7

When in (Ancient) Rome

Ancient Rome had its own system for collecting taxes. The Romans taxed people in many different ways. One tax—called a head tax—was an equal amount of money that every citizen had to pay. Paying taxes was hard for some people, but the Roman government used these taxes to support its empire.

One way the Romans used taxes was to build roads and bridges. Their road system made it easier to trade with far-off lands. It also made it easier to spread news throughout the empire.

Roman city planners also used taxes to build aqueducts, or water pipes. Aqueducts made it easier for people to get fresh, clean water. They also carried away dirty water that had unhealthy germs in it. Without taxes, ancient Romans wouldn't have had the benefits of clean water and useful roads.

Some Ancient Roman roads are still around today, thousands of years later.

compareandcontrast

Head taxes were equal for each person. Why might this kind of tax be harder on poorer people than a tithe?

Roman aqueducts still stand today.

The Fight for Representation

Taxes became a key source of money for governments. Taxes benefitted people in some ways. However, people weren't always happy about paying taxes. One example of this was the people in the American colonies more than 250 years ago.

Before the 1760s, the American colonies had a lot of freedom. However, they were still colonies of Great Britain, and the British government ruled over them. They wanted the freedom to make choices about how they lived.

Great Britain ruled its 13 American colonies from across the ocean, making laws that colonists had to follow.

The people who founded the colonies had left England to start a new life.

In 1765, the British Parliament forced the colonies to pay new taxes. The Parliament was the group that made laws in Great Britain. The American colonists thought Parliament was not treating them fairly. The colonists were angry about "taxation without **representation**." That means they had to pay taxes to Great Britain but had no one to represent them in British Parliament.

WORD WISE

Representation means the people living under a government get to participate in making the laws or rules they must follow.

Stamp Act Protests

The Stamp Act was passed in 1765, forcing colonists to put a stamp on printed items such as legal papers and newspapers. They had to buy this stamp from the British government. The Stamp Act made the colonists angry. They refused to buy the stamps.

Representatives from nine colonies had a meeting. They wrote a list of the reasons why they didn't like the tax. They asked the British government to take back the law. Merchants in the colonies also agreed not to buy items from Great Britain. That meant people in Great Britain could not sell things they made to people in the colonies. Great Britain lost money.

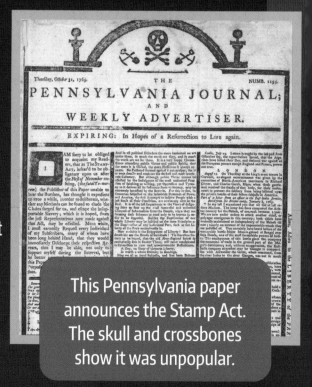

This Pennsylvania paper announces the Stamp Act. The skull and crossbones show it was unpopular.

This illustration shows protests against the Stamp Act.

Because of the protests, the British Parliament ended the tax in 1766. The Stamp Act had helped bring the colonists together. It was just the beginning of unrest and protest in the colonies.

Consider This

What are some reasons the colonists might have been in favor of boycotting, or not buying, certain goods from Great Britain? How might it benefit them?

The Unpopular Townshend Acts

Though the Stamp Act ended, it wasn't the end of unpopular British taxation. Soon after, a British official named Charles Townshend got Parliament to pass several new tax laws. The Townshend Acts were four laws that angered the colonists even more. One of the acts taxed tea, lead, paint, paper, and glass coming into colonial ports. These products were important for helping to build new homes, towns, and businesses in the colonies. Furthermore, the colonists still did not have representation in Parliament.

A Black sailor named Crispus Attucks was the first person shot during the Boston Massacre.

One reason the Boston Massacre happened is because thousands of British soldiers were in Boston.

One of the Townshend Acts even let British spies check to make sure colonists paid the taxes. To keep order, the British government sent soldiers to Boston, Massachusetts, in 1768. On March 5, 1770, a group of British soldiers tried to calm down angry colonists. The colonists shouted and threw things at the soldiers. The soldiers shot their guns at the crowd. Five colonists were killed, which angered colonists greatly. Called the Boston Massacre, it was one step closer to revolution.

Can you think of some drawbacks to being ruled by a country far away? Can you think of any benefits to it?

15

Intolerable Acts

The Townshend Acts were repealed, or done away with, soon after the Boston Massacre. However, the tax on tea stayed in place. Then, in 1773, Parliament passed the Tea Act, which allowed a British company to sell tea at a lower price than American companies.

On December 16, 1773, American colonists boarded British ships in Boston Harbor. They threw the British tea into the water to protest the taxes. This event became known as the Boston Tea Party.

The Boston Tea Party showed the anger that American colonists had over the Tea Act.

The Declaration of Independence told the British king, and the world, that the colonies would now be independent, or free, states.

The British government passed new laws. The colonists called them the **Intolerable** Acts. They were a punishment for the Boston Tea Party. The laws said the colonists had to pay for the tea they ruined. The colonies banded together against these unfair acts. By July 4, 1776, the Declaration of Independence was signed, and the American Revolution was underway.

WORD WISE

Intolerable means unbearable. The laws passed by Great Britain were so unfair that the American colonists couldn't put up with them.

Taxes Are Important

Why do we need taxes today? What exactly do they pay for? The government uses the money collected by its citizens to pay for what it needs. Governments collect taxes for many reasons. The most important one is to pay for services. One example of these services is an army or police officers to protect people. Another example of government services is building roads and bridges, just as the ancient Romans did. Keeping these roads and bridges in good shape also takes a lot of money.

Without taxes, the government may not be able to keep up bridges and roads that help people travel.

Governments may put high taxes on cigarettes to help people stop smoking.

Some governments use taxes to try to change people's behavior. Many states have used taxes to try to make people avoid unhealthy food or soda. Businesses sometimes pay higher taxes if the products they make are unhealthy in some way. One tax, sometimes called a "soda tax," aims to lessen the amount of sugary drinks people consume.

Consider This

Do you think it's right for a government to put higher taxes on unhealthy foods, drinks, and products?

Taxes for Work

When you work, you may think that you get to keep every dollar you make. However, almost everyone who works in the United States pays some type of tax. A tax on the money made at one's job is called an **income** tax. A tax on the money that people make is called a personal income tax. Businesses also pay taxes on the money they make. They pay a corporate income tax.

Companies in the United States often take some of a worker's income and send the money straight to the federal government. Some states also collect their own tax on income.

People must send in their tax forms and payments to the government between January and April each year.

Income tax is used to help pay for national services such as the mail.

The more money you earn, the more taxes you must pay. The Internal Revenue Service (IRS) is the agency in charge of taxes. Every year it collects income taxes from American workers. People have to tell the IRS how much they make per year to see how much they owe.

WORD WISE

Any of the money that somebody earns from work, business, or his or her property is called income.

Taxes for Your Community

Federal taxes help pay to keep larger government services running. However, taxes are also collected and used by smaller communities, such as states, counties, and towns. These taxes help pay for programs that help the people who live in those communities.

If the citizens in a county or state care about having good schools, they can vote for more taxes that will pay for better schools.

Without state-funded healthcare, some people wouldn't be able to go to the doctor.

Some state taxes pay for health care. This helps pay for people who can't afford to see the doctor or buy medicine on their own. State governments collect the taxes from everybody. Then they give some of the money to those people who need it.

Local taxes can also be used to give money to schools. In every community there are public schools that children can go to for free. Public schools are usually supported by state, county, and local taxes. The more money these schools get, the more they can spend on teachers, staff, supplies, and programs.

Consider This

What are some places or services in your town that might be paid for with local taxes?

Taxes When You Shop

When shopping, it's smart to think about how much something will cost once the sales tax is added. Then you know what you can afford. Imagine you have five dollars and you want a toy that costs four dollars. Add the sales tax to see if you have enough money.

Next time you buy something, look at your receipt to see the amount of sales tax you paid.

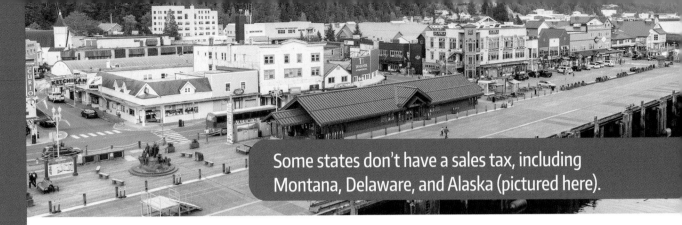

Some states don't have a sales tax, including Montana, Delaware, and Alaska (pictured here).

Some products may be exempt from sales tax, which means they are not taxed. They are usually basic needs, such as food and education. In the United States, sales tax is often added to the price of something when you pay for it. That is why some things cost more than the amount on the price tag. In some European countries, taxes are included in the price.

Sales taxes can be set aside for special purposes. For example, taxes from the gas people put in their cars are often used to pay for fixing roads or for public transportation. This benefits the community that uses these modes of transportation.

Consider This

Some states offer tax-free days before school starts to help people afford school supplies. What supplies do you think should be tax-free? Why?

Understanding Tariffs

When products go from one country to another, tariffs are collected. These special taxes are also called duties or customs. The most common kind of tariff is an import tariff. An import tariff is a tax on **foreign** businesses that want to sell their goods in a country. An export tariff is a tax on a country's own businesses. Companies must pay the government before sending their goods out of the country to sell. Transit tariffs are taxes on goods passing through one country on their way to another country.

Many imports and exports come in and out of U.S. ports, such as this one.

Tariffs differ based on the product. Some goods have no tariff, while some have high tariffs.

Tariffs have existed since the Middle Ages. Countries often charge higher tariffs during hard times, such as war. When the economy is good, tariffs become less common. Some countries have agreements with each other not to collect tariffs. These deals increase trade. Government leaders have to meet to make trade and tariff agreements that are good for their country.

WORD WISE

When something is considered foreign, it means it comes from somewhere outside of our own country.

Other Ways to Raise Money

Raising taxes is often unpopular. How can governments raise more money without raising taxes? There are a few other ways, such as lotteries. A lottery is a gambling game. A large number of people buy tickets in hopes of winning a prize. Sometimes the money raised in a lottery is used for special projects or important programs.

While lotteries can raise money, taxes bring in the most money for governments. Some taxes are the same for everyone. Some taxes are different based on how much money you earn. Many people argue about taxes. Some people want higher taxes on big companies. Some people want fewer taxes across the board. Understanding what taxes are and how they're used can help you become a good citizen.

compare and contrast

Can you think of similarities and differences
between taxes and lotteries?

Glossary

ancient: Relating to a time early in history.

citizens: The people who are full members of a country, state, or town.

colonies: A group of people from one country who live in a new territory but keep ties with the parent state.

customs: Another name for taxes paid on imports or exports.

duties: Another name for taxes paid on imports or exports.

empire: A large territory or a number of territories or peoples, under a single authority.

exempt: Free from a requirement to which others are subject.

gambling: Relating to games where one bets on an uncertain outcome.

government: The people, laws, and customs that rule over a country.

income: Money earned from work, business, or property owned.

massacre: The killing of a number of helpless human beings.

merchant: A buyer and seller of goods.

Middle Ages: The period of European history from about 500 CE to 1500 CE.

ports: Harbor towns or cities where ships load or unload cargo.

protest: To object or show some type of disagreement.

services: Useful work or groups that provide for some type of public need.

value: The amount of money that something is worth.

For More Information

Books

Boothroyd, Jennifer. *Taxes*. Minneapolis, MN: Bearport Publishing Company, 2023.

Lawton, Cassie M. *Taxes*. New York, NY: Cavendish Square Publishing, 2021.

Websites

Taxes
www.ducksters.com/history/us_government/taxes.php
Learn more about different kinds of taxes and how they're used.

Taxes: U.S. Government for Kids
www.coolkidfacts.com/taxes-us-government/
Discover the history behind taxes and how they're used.

Index

A

American Revolution, 17
aqueducts, 8, 9
army, 18

B

Boston Massacre, 14,
    15, 16
Boston Tea Party, 16, 17
bridges, 7, 8, 9, 18

C

corvée, 7
crops, 6, 7

D

driver's license, 5

E

England, 11g

F

food, 19, 25
freedom, 10

G

gas, 25

H

head tax, 8, 9
healthcare, 23

I

income tax, 20, 21
Internal Revenue Service,
    21
Intolerable Acts, 17

L

land, 6, 7
local taxes, 23
lotteries, 28, 29

M

mail, 21

P

police officers, 4, 18

R

roads, 7, 8, 9, 18, 25
Rome, 8, 9, 18

S

sales tax, 4, 24, 25
schools, 22, 23, 29
Stamp Act, 12, 13, 14

T

tariffs, 26, 27
taxation without
    representation, 11
Tea Act, 16
tithe, 6, 7
Townshend Acts, 14, 15, 16